green press INITIATIVE

Nomad Press is committed to preserving ancient forests and natural resources.
We elected to print *Explore Simple Machines!* on 100% post consumer recycled paper,
processed chlorine free. As a result, for this printing, we have saved:

24 Trees, (equal to half an American football field)
22,958 Gallons of water, (equal to a shower of 4.8 days)
7,544 Pounds of air emissions, (equal to emissions of 1 car per year)

Nomad Press made this paper choice because our printer, Transcontinental, is a member of
Green Press Initiative, a nonprofit program dedicated to supporting authors, publishers,
and suppliers in their efforts to reduce their use of fiber obtained from endangered forests.

For more information, visit www.greenpressinitiative.org

Nomad Press
A division of Nomad Communications
10 9 8 7 6 5 4 3 2 1

This book was manufactured by Transcontinental Gagné,
Louiseville Québec, Canada
August 2011, Job #49274
ISBN: 978-1-936313-82-2

Illustrations by Bryan Stone
Educational Consultant, Marla Conn

Questions regarding the ordering of this book should be addressed to
Independent Publishers Group
814 N. Franklin St.
Chicago, IL 60610
www.ipgbook.com

Nomad Press
2456 Christian St.
White River Junction, VT 05001
www.nomadpress.net

CONTENTS

1   Introduction

4   Chapter 1: Simply Helpful

12   Chapter 2: Levers

26   Chapter 3: Inclined Planes

34   Chapter 4: Wheels and Axles

46   Chapter 5: Screws

57   Chapter 6: Wedges

68   Chapter 7: Pulleys

80   Chapter 8: Be an Inventor

Glossary O Resources O Index

Titles in the **Explore** Your World! Series

INTRODUCTION

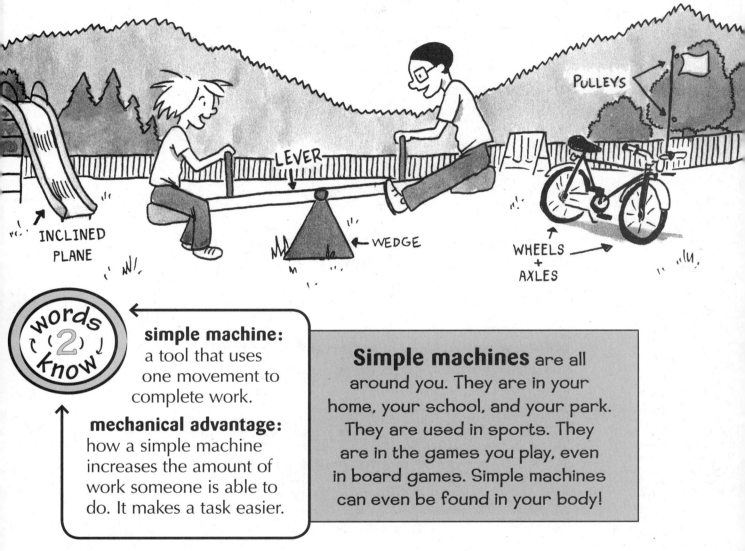

PULLEYS

LEVER

INCLINED PLANE

WEDGE

WHEELS + AXLES

words 2 know

simple machine: a tool that uses one movement to complete work.

mechanical advantage: how a simple machine increases the amount of work someone is able to do. It makes a task easier.

Simple machines are all around you. They are in your home, your school, and your park. They are used in sports. They are in the games you play, even in board games. Simple machines can even be found in your body!

Simple machines by themselves have few or no moving parts. They help us to pull, push, lift, and divide. Your muscle power—not electricity or gasoline—makes them work. Simple machines can't do all the work, but they make things easier! This is called a **mechanical advantage**.

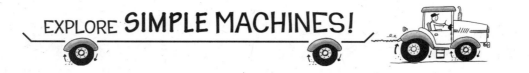

THERE ARE SIX TYPES OF SIMPLE MACHINES:

* **lever:** a bar that rests on a support and lifts or moves things.

* **inclined plane:** a flat surface that connects a lower level to a higher level.

* **wheel and axle:** a wheel with a rod that turn together to lift and move loads. The axle is the rod around which the wheel rotates.

* **screw:** an inclined plane or lever wrapped around a pole that pulls one thing toward another.

* **wedge:** an object with slanted sides ending in a sharp edge that lifts or splits another object.

* **pulley:** grooved wheels with ropes used to lift something or change its direction.

COMMON THINGS THAT ARE SIMPLE MACHINES

↔ Shovels are levers that can help you loosen and move dirt.

↔ Ramps are inclined planes used for carts and wheelchairs.

↔ School buses need wheels and axles to roll.

↔ Lids are screws that seal jar openings.

↔ Zippers are wedges that fasten your coat.

↔ School flags are raised by pulleys.

INTRODUCTION

Most machines include more than one simple machine. These are called **compound machines**. A wagon is a compound machine. It has four wheels and two axles. The handle is a lever. Some compound machines are quite complex with many working parts, such as bulldozers or cars. Compound machines can be found in factories that make the things we use every day. They can even help us explore space and the oceans!

compound machine: two or more simple machines working together.

In this book you will be asked to look for simple machines in your home. You will figure out how they work and why they do the things they do. You'll get to do lots of fun experiments and projects. Plus, you'll learn some silly jokes and a lot of amazing facts. So get ready to Explore Simple Machines!

? DID ? YOU KNOW

People have been using simple machines since ancient times. They used them in spears and in bows and arrows to hunt, on boats to move from place to place, and on the farm to plow and harvest crops. Simple machines were even used to build fantastic structures like the Egyptian pyramids and the Roman Coliseum!

SIMPLY HELPFUL

FORCES MAKE THINGS MOVE.

Moving a heavy bag of sand with your bare hands is a tough job. But what if you had a simple machine to help? Then you could push the bag up a plank of wood, move it with a wheelbarrow, or lift it with a shovel. By changing the power, speed, or direction of a movement, simple machines make your **work** easier.

In science, the term "work" does not mean homework. "Work" is a **force** that moves an object a distance. For example, you did work when you picked up this book. You did more work when you flipped the pages. Whenever you lift, **push** or **pull** something, you are doing work.

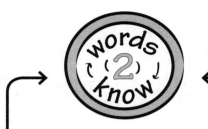

FORCES

To understand how simple machines make our work easier, you need to understand forces. You don't have to be in a movie for the force to be with you. The world is full of them! A simple push or pull is a force. You push on a door to open it. You pull on a door to close it shut behind you.

When you are standing still, the pushing and pulling forces are balanced. In science this balance is called **equilibrium**. There is no movement because the forces are equal.

But when forces are not equal, they are **unbalanced**. This creates movement. If you play tug of war against a team of equal strength, the rope does not move much. But if one team is much stronger, the rope moves. You could say that the forces acting on the rope are not equal.

work: a force that moves an object a distance.

force: a push or a pull.

push: a force that moves something away from you.

pull: a force that brings something towards you.

equilibrium: when forces are balanced.

unbalanced: when two forces are not equal. This causes motion.

Imagine standing at the top of a mountain with a snowboard strapped to your feet. Ready to try some jumps and tricks, you push off. You turn, twist, spin, and balance. How did you do this? With the help of force! Forces cannot be seen, but they can move you forwards and backwards. They can move you up and down. They can change your direction. They can speed you up, slow you down, and even stop you.

STOP MOVING!

In order to move an object, simple machines must overcome **gravity** and **friction**. Gravity is a force pulling you and every other object towards Earth. It gives objects **weight**.

Friction is also a force—a force trying to stop you from moving! Whether you are rollerblading down the street or zooming down a skateboard ramp, friction is working to slow you down. Friction slows two objects down when they rub against each together—like bike wheels rubbing against the ground. Friction does this by moving in the opposite direction from the object in motion.

Imagine putting on ice skates only to find that the ice has been replaced with sand! Besides being no fun, the sand would slow you down. Rough surfaces like sand or grass create more friction than smooth surfaces like ice or concrete.

words 2 know

gravity: a force that pulls all objects to the earth.

friction: the force that resists motion between two objects in contact.

weight: a measure of the force of gravity on an object.

Try This

Get a straight drinking straw. Balance the straw on your finger until you find its center of gravity. Don't allow it to tilt. You'll find that the straw can balance when the force of gravity pulls equally on both sides. When the forces of gravity are unbalanced, the straw falls.

words (2) know

lubricant: a substance, like oil or grease, that reduces friction.

Newton: a unit used to measure the amount of force you need to move something.

Can you think of a way to fight friction? If you said try harder, you're right! In order to move, you have to push harder than the force of the friction. You could also apply a **lubricant**, like oil. Lubricants reduce friction.

Friction isn't all bad. It can cause a positive change too. Without friction, lots of things you take for granted, like walking, would be impossible. When you walk, friction "grips" the soles of your shoes. Without friction, you would just slide around until you fell down!

HOW IS FORCE MEASURED?

When you throw a baseball you use force. That force is measured in **Newtons**. One Newton is 3½ ounces (100 grams), or about the weight of an apple.

This measurement is named after a scientist, Sir Isaac Newton. Newton lived about 300 years ago. He was very interested in how and why things move. He discovered how gravity works.

MAKE YOUR OWN JOURNAL

SUPPLIES

→ cereal box

→ scissors

→ brown paper bag

→ white glue

→ found paper like graph paper, loose leaf, or stationery

→ hole puncher

→ dental floss

→ needle

→ magazines and newspapers

A science journal is an important place where you can record your observations and make notes. Now you can make a journal to keep track of what you see and discover in this book.

1 Cut your cereal box so it opens like a book. Cut across the top and bottom, following the fold.

2 Cut the brown paper bag into two 6-by-8-inch pieces (15 by 20 centimeters).

3 Apply white glue to the outside of the cereal box and attach the brown paper. Set to one side to dry.

4 From the found paper, cut journal pages to 5 by 7½ inches (12 by 19 centimeters). You need enough to fill the cereal box cover.

A simple machine only works if you supply the energy. Energy allows you to move things. A knife will lie on the counter until you pick it up and push it through an apple. Then the knife will move in the direction of your force.

5 Use the hole puncher to make three holes, about 1 inch (2½ centimeters) in from the edge on your found papers. The holes go on the left of your journal.

6 Put the paper inside your journal's cover. Take a pencil and mark where the holes should go on the cover.

7 Punch matching holes in the front and back covers of your journal.

8 Thread a needle with dental floss and push it through the holes in the paper and the cover. When you are finished going in and out of each hole, secure the dental floss by tying it.

9 From magazines and newspapers, cut out images of simple machines. Glue them to your cover. Leave a space on your journal cover for your name.

Just for **LAUGHS!**

WHY DID THE SIMPLE MACHINE STOP WORKING?
It didn't have the energy!

FRICTION EXPERIMENT

SUPPLIES

→ toy car

→ baking sheet or tray

→ books

→ stopwatch

→ cardboard

→ sandpaper

→ dish towel

→ carpet

→ journal

Friction is a force. It resists the movement between two objects that are touching. You can create different amounts of friction between the baking sheet and car by using different surfaces.

1 Before you begin, write down in your journal which material you think it will be easiest for the toy car to move over— the cardboard, sandpaper, dish towel, or carpet.

2 Set up a gentle slope by placing a baking sheet at an angle on a book.

3 Place the toy car on top and let it roll down. Use your stopwatch to record the time.

4 Repeat the experiment by placing each material, one at a time, on the baking sheet surface and letting the car roll down.

5 Write down your observations and conclusions in your journal.

WHAT'S HAPPENING?

↑ Friction is a force that can change motion. Different surfaces have different amounts of friction. Smoother surfaces have less friction than rough surfaces.

MAKE YOUR OWN MOBILE

A mobile is a piece of art with objects dangling from strings. All the parts of a mobile must balance. Try this activity to find out how to balance a mobile. An adult needs to help with the wire cutters.

SUPPLIES

→ wire coat hanger

→ wire cutters

→ yarn

→ bottles, lids, and scrap materials

→ journal

1 Bend a wire coat hanger to make a circle. Ask an adult to snip off the hook with wire cutters. Wrap yarn around the wire to completely cover it.

2 Tie four pieces of 15-inch yarn to the circle (38 centimeters). The strings need to be evenly spaced. Gather the ends of the yarn together at the top.

3 Hang the mobile from a low hook and adjust the yarn strings to make it balance.

4 Select objects to tie to your mobile. If the mobile does not balance, keep experimenting with the objects until you can balance the mobile.

5 Write down the results in your journal.

THINGS TO DISCUSS

↑ When the mobile is level and balanced, what must be true of the forces acting on it?

↑ When the mobile is unbalanced, what must be true of the forces acting on it?

↑ If you change the length of the mobile strings, does this affect your results?

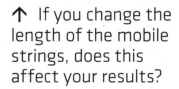

LEVERS

A LEVER IS A BAR THAT RESTS ON A SUPPORT TO LIFT OR MOVE THINGS.

Have you ever hit a baseball? Or played a piano? Then you've used levers. Levers are one of the most common simple machines. Levers aren't just for playing, though. They're also for work! People can move objects many times heavier than their own weight with the help of a lever. And some types of levers are even in your body. You use levers when you stand on your tiptoes, throw a baseball, or nod your head.

Do you like to play on a seesaw? If one of your friends sits down on one end, you shoot up into the air. This makes you an important part of a lever!

LEVERS

fulcrum: the point on which a lever turns or pivots.

load: the object you are moving in your work.

effort: the force that is used on a simple machine to move the load.

engineer: someone who designs or builds things such as roads, bridges, and buildings.

Levers have four parts: the bar, the **fulcrum**, the **load**, and the **effort**. The bar is the plank you sit on. It rests on the fulcrum. The fulcrum does not move. That's the center of the seesaw. The load is the name for what is lifted. That's you. The effort is the energy put into lifting something. That's your friend sitting down on the other side.

There are three different ways to arrange the fulcrum, load, and effort. This creates three different types or classes of levers. Each class of lever has a different use. Let's take a closer look.

CLASS ONE LEVER: An **engineer** in ancient Rome who wanted to lift a heavy stone block might have used a class one lever. This kind of lever is like a seesaw. The fulcrum is between the load and the effort. If the effort is down then the load is up. Moving the load closer to the fulcrum makes lifting a heavy object easier.

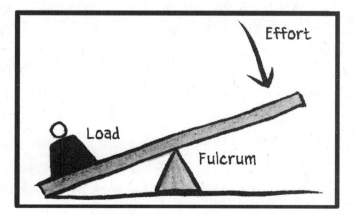

Pliers are an example of a class one lever. Scissors are another. The fulcrum is the point in the middle that connects the two blades of the scissors. The effort is squeezing your hands to move the blades. What you are cutting is the load.

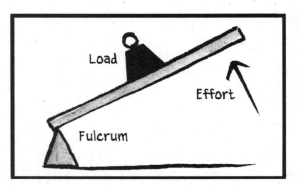

WOW!!

Ancient scissors have been found in Egyptian ruins that are 3,500 years old. They look like the letter U. The curve acted as a spring and the blades did not cross. Modern cross-blade scissors were invented by the ancient Romans 2,000 years ago. They have two blades that pivot around a fulcrum.

CLASS TWO LEVER: A class two lever has the load between the effort and the fulcrum. This type of lever is used to move heavy loads. Dump trucks and wheelbarrows are class two levers. Can you guess which part of a wheelbarrow is the fulcrum? It's the wheel. The effort is your hands lifting the handles.

CLASS THREE LEVER: This lever has the effort in between the fulcrum and the load. Most of the levers found in your body are class three levers. When you throw a ball, you use a class three lever: your arm! Class three levers increase the speed and distance an object travels.

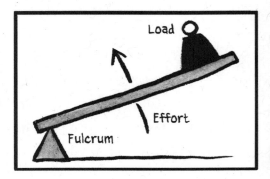

LEVERS

Try This

Grab your journal and a digital camera. Take a walk around your home, garage, or school. Try to find as many levers as you can. Take a picture of each. Identify what jobs they do. Try to find the fulcrum. Describe in your journal how you think the levers work.

WORKING TOGETHER

Sometimes levers are joined together with **linkages**. A linkage is a joint or link that connects two or more levers together. When one lever moves, its motion is passed on to the next lever and so on.

words 2 know

linkage: a link that connects two or more levers together.

Have you ever played the game "Pass the Squeeze?" In this game, you hold hands in a circle of people, and when your hand gets squeezed, you then squeeze your neighbor's hand. Slowly the squeeze is passed around the circle. Linkages are a lot like this.

Linkages are all around you. Your bicycle uses linkages. When you squeeze the brake lever, a series of linkages sends the force to the brakes on the wheels. Now that's working together!

? DID YOU KNOW

There are many levers in your body like fingers and toes. When a muscle tightens, the bone it is attached to acts as a lever. The joint is the fulcrum. This makes your body move!

LEVERS IN HISTORY

The first person to figure out how levers worked was Archimedes. This Greek engineer and scientist lived more than 2,000 years ago. He realized that the longer the arm of the lever, the less force was needed to move an object. "Give me a lever long enough," he said, "and I will move the earth." Gradually people began using levers for many purposes including **agriculture**, construction, and **defense**.

agriculture: growing plants, called crops, for food.

defense: protecting against danger.

invent: to be the first to think of or make something new.

shaduf: an Egyptian device used to raise water.

counterweight: an object used to balance another object.

irrigation ditch: a narrow channel dug in the ground to move water.

AGRICULTURE

Carrying water, bucket by bucket, is exhausting work. So the ancient Egyptians **invented** the **shaduf** almost 4,000 years ago. A shaduf is a giant class one lever with a bucket on one end of a pole and a **counterweight** on the other. The pole rests on a large stand.

To work the shaduf, a person lowers the bucket into the water. When the bucket is full, it is easily lifted up with the help of the heavy weight on the other end of the pole. The bucket can then be swung around and emptied. Egyptians used the shaduf to lift water from the Nile river into **irrigation ditches** that watered crops.

LEVERS

? DID YOU KNOW
The shaduf is still used in many parts of Africa and Asia. A shaduf can raise about 600 gallons of water a day (2,271 liters).

CONSTRUCTION

Today, construction companies rely on complex machines. Cranes are used to move heavy objects. In the past, levers were used to lift and move stones into place. Wooden rods were shoved under the stone to be moved. A person applied force to one end of the rod by pushing down on it. The rod transferred the energy to the stone, making it lift up. This process might have to be repeated again and again until the stone was in the correct place.

Around the world, there are amazing examples of buildings built with help from levers. In Italy, there is the Coliseum. In France, there is the Notre Dame Cathedral. And in South America, there is the Peruvian city of Machu Picchu

words 2 know

archaeologist: a scientist who studies ancient people through the objects they left behind.

found high in the Andes. **Archaeologists** believe workers at Machu Picchu used a system of inclined planes and levers to push granite stones into place.

DEFENSE

Archimedes put the lever to use defending the ancient Greek city of Syracuse. He built a **catapult**, a machine that can lift things and send them flying! In this case it threw massive boulders at the invading Roman forces. Thanks to Archimedes' weapons, the city of Syracuse avoided capture for almost a year.

The lever was still being used in war 1,500 years later, in the form of a **trebuchet**. This is a class one lever used to throw heavy objects at castles and cities. A trebuchet had a huge lever arm. Some could measure over 59 feet long (18 meters)!

words 2 know

catapult: a large war machine used to hurl objects at an enemy.

trebuchet: a weapon used to throw heavy objects to destroy castles and cities.

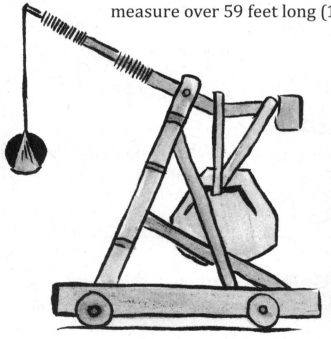

WOW!!

Levers are even used in outer space. Astronauts use a 55-foot-long robotic arm (17 meters) called Canadarm to launch and grab satellites, and do repairs in space. Canadarm works just like a human arm, but it can lift more than the bulk of the entire space shuttle!

LEVERS

Just for LAUGHS!

WHY DID THE LEVER CHANGE DIRECTION?
Because it reached its turning point!

ANIMALS USE TOOLS!

Animals use levers to get work done. Sea otters use rocks to open abalone shells. Elephants use sticks to scratch their bodies. Chimpanzees make their own tools too. First they find a sturdy stick. Then they peel the bark off to make it more usable. Chimpanzees use their new tool to fish out tasty termites from a log or termite mound.

THEN & NOW

Then: The first vending machine was invented by a man named Hero of Alexandria, who lived in Egypt almost 2,000 years ago. The machine let out water when a coin was dropped through a slot. The coin dropped onto a pan that lifted a lever stopping the water.

Now: Vending machines run on motors. They sell everything from stamps to soda.

SUPPLIES

→ jumping jack template from page 22

→ cereal box

→ pencil

→ ruler

→ scissors

→ hole puncher

→ 4 brass fasteners

→ string

→ colored markers

A jumping jack is a puppet that is usually made from wood with strings connecting the joints. It is one of the earliest types of mechanical toys to use levers. The arms and legs of the puppet move up and down when the string is pulled. Try this activity to make your own jumping jack.

1 Copy and cut out the jumping jack template. Cut the cereal box so that the cardboard lies flat.

2 With the inside of the cereal box facing you, trace around the jumping jack template from page 22. You will need 1 body rectangle and 4 arm/leg rectangles.

3 Using the hole puncher, make two holes near the top of each arm/leg rectangle and a hole in each corner of the body rectangle. Use your templates for hole placement.

4 Line up the lower hole on the arm rectangles to the holes on the body. Secure with fasteners. Your arms are now in place. Loop a piece of string through the top holes.

5 Attach the legs in the same way with the brass fasteners. Loop another string through these top holes.

6 Tie a long piece of string so it connects the top and bottom string. Let the extra string hang down.

WHAT GAME NEEDS A ROCK, PAPER, AND A LEVER?
Rock, Paper, Scissors!

7 Color your jumping jack with a silly outfit. Get creative!

8 Pull down on the string and watch your toy move.

VARIATION

↑ Draw and cut out a head, hands, and feet for your jumping jack. You can attach them by cutting holes with the hole puncher and using more brass fasteners.

WOW!!

Easter Island is famous for its hundreds of huge stone statues called Moai. Archaeologists do not know exactly how these Moai were put into place. One theory is that the people of Easter Island used levers to raise the statues, some of which are 13 feet high (4 meters) and weigh as much as 14 tons (12¾ metric tons)!

21

JUMPING JACK TEMPLATE

Use the shapes below to make your Jumping Jack.

BODY (you will need 1)

ARM/LEG (you will need 4)

LET'S LIFT WITH LEVERS

Levers lift and move objects. In this activity, explore how a lever can take a force like your push and make it bigger.

1 Try to lift a book with two fingers. Write down what happened.

2 Now place the paper towel roll on a flat surface. This is your fulcrum. Secure either end to the surface with masking tape to keep the tube from rolling.

3 Place the yard/meter stick on top of the roll so that the 24-inch mark (61 centimeters) is over the roll. The yard/meter stick must be perpendicular to the roll.

4 Place the book on the short end of the stick and press on the other end to lift the book.

5 Try this experiment again, only this time move the roll closer to the book. Repeat step 4.

THINGS TO DISCUSS

↑ Was it easier to lift the book with two fingers or with the lever?

↑ How did the lever make your push bigger?

↑ Did you use less, more, or the same amount of force to lift the book when you moved the roll closer to it.

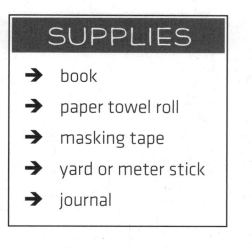

CHOPSTICK CHALLENGE

SUPPLIES

→ group of friends

→ 4 cereal bowls

→ 20 sugar cubes

→ 2 sets of chopsticks

When two chopsticks are used together they become a class one lever. To use chopsticks, hold them at the top between your thumb and index finger, middle finger, and third finger. Your index and middle finger control the chopsticks.

1 Make two equal teams. Give each team one empty bowl, one bowl with 10 sugar cubes in it, and one pair of chopsticks.

2 Ask an adult to say, "Go." Each person takes a turn transferring all of the sugar cubes from a full bowl to an empty bowl. The first team to have all their players complete this challenge, wins.

WHAT'S HAPPENING?

↑ A class one lever like chopsticks takes a small movement and makes it bigger. This is why you only have to press down lightly on a pair of chopsticks to pick up a tiny object like a grain of rice or a larger object like a piece of sushi.

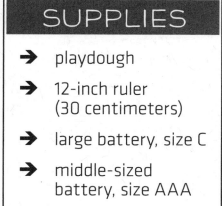

MAKE A CLASS ONE LEVER

In a class one lever, the fulcrum separates the effort and the load. In this activity, investigate the connection between the effort, the load, and the fulcrum.

1 Build a lever by first rolling a piece of playdough into a ball and placing it on the table. This will be your fulcrum.

2 Center the ruler on top of the playdough. Place the batteries on opposite ends of the ruler.

3 Try to think of ways to balance the batteries. Write your results in your journal. Here is a hint: You can try moving the location of the batteries or the playdough.

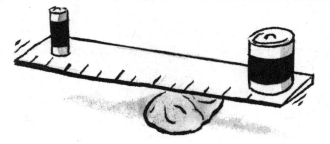

VARIATION

↑ What happens if you move your load (the smaller battery) closer to the fulcrum?

↑ What happens if you move the fulcrum closer to the load?

THEN & NOW

Then: Ancient Egyptians fashioned hammers by fixing a stone between two wooden sticks held together by a leather strap.

Now: Hammers are made from metal. The handle, which is the lever, is still often made from wood.

INCLINED PLANES

AN INCLINED PLANE IS A FLAT SURFACE THAT CONNECTS A LOWER LEVEL WITH A HIGHER LEVEL.

What happens when you build a skateboard park without any ramps? Absolutely nothing, of course! When it comes to having fun on a skateboard, you have to have ramps. They allow skaters to get big air and do cool tricks.

Did you know that a skateboard ramp is a simple machine? Inclined planes come in many forms, such as ramps, slides, stairs, winding roads, and escalators.

26

INCLINED PLANES

Imagine walking straight up a steep mountain. It would be a hard job. A winding road or path would take longer but you would use less effort. Remember the force of gravity? An inclined plane splits gravity into two smaller forces. When you use an inclined plane like a winding road, you go forwards and up. The distance you travel is greater but the force is less.

Ancient Egyptians used inclined planes to build the pyramids. The largest pyramid in the world is the Great Pyramid of Giza. It was built for the pharaoh Khufu around 2560 **BCE** and contains more than two million stone blocks. Each block weighs between 2½ and 15 tons (2¼ and 13½ metric tons)! How was the Great Pyramid built? No one knows exactly. The ancient Egyptians may have used earth and mud bricks to make ramps.

? DID YOU KNOW

In ancient times, armies built inclined planes called siege ramps. These ramps made it possible for armies to haul heavy equipment to the tops of high walls. In 73 **CE**, Roman soldiers built a huge siege ramp using thousands of tons of dirt and rock to attack the hilltop Jewish settlement of Masada. The ramp still exists today!

WATER TRANSPORTATION

Rivers and lakes have always been important for transportation. But sometimes there is a big difference in water levels between two bodies of water, blocking ships and boats from moving forward.

To solve this problem, the **lock** was invented. A lock is a fixed chamber with gates at either end. The boat enters the lock and the gate is closed. Then the water level is raised or lowered to the height of the next body of water. But the locks were slow and wasted lots of water.

words 2 know

lock: an enclosure in a canal with gates at each end used to raise or lower boats as they pass from one level to another.

skeleton: a winter sport in which a driver rides head first on a sled.

SPORTY INCLINED PLANES

Inclined planes help us play sports. Have you ever watched the Winter Olympics on television? Some sports, like skiing, depend on the natural inclined plane of a mountain. Others sports, like bobsled, luge, and **skeleton**, depend on inclined planes built by people. In skeleton, for example, athletes lie on a sled about the size of a doormat and zoom head first down an icy manmade track at speeds of more than 60 miles per hour (96 kilometers)!

INCLINED PLANES

In the late eighteenth century, people realized that these problems could be overcome with inclined planes. Instead of entering a fixed chamber, the boat enters a moveable chamber filled with water, and then the entire chamber is lifted up or down an inclined plane. For example, the Saint-Louis-Arzviller inclined plane is located on the Marne-Rhine Canal in France. The change in water level is 146 feet (44½ meters). Before the construction of the incline, it took boats 8 to 13 hours to travel 2 miles (4 kilometers) through 17 locks. After the incline opened, it only took 4 minutes!

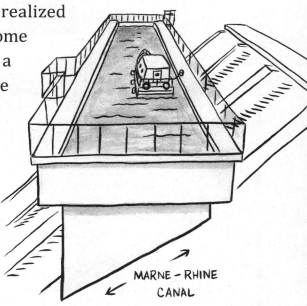

MARNE – RHINE CANAL

words 2 know

switchback: a road that zigzags back and forth.

ascent: the way up.

descent: the way down.

A CHALLENGE!

What's the world's most challenging road? It could be the Stelvio Pass in the Italian Alps. At 9,045 feet (2,757 meters), it is one of the highest roads in Europe. Because it was built on the side of a very steep mountain, the Stelvio Pass has 48 narrow hairpin curves that make the road drivable. These zigzagging curves are called **switchbacks**. This type of inclined plane reduces the work of a car's engine by allowing for an easier **ascent** or **descent**. Even so, sometimes drivers can't see the oncoming traffic!

MAKE YOUR OWN
ICE CREAM

SUPPLIES

→ liquid measuring cup

→ ¼ cup whole milk (60 milliliters)

→ ¼ teaspoon vanilla extract

→ 1 teaspoon sugar (5 milliliters)

→ plastic ziploc sandwich bag

→ 2 cups ice (500 milliliters)

→ ½ cup rock salt (120 milliliters)

→ quart-sized plastic ziploc bag

→ newspaper

→ metal coffee can with lid

→ wooden board

→ stack of books or a chair

Try the following activity to find out how to make ice cream using an inclined plane.

1 Pour the milk and vanilla into the measuring cup. Pour the sugar into the small plastic bag.

2 Slowly add the milk and vanilla to the sugar. Carefully seal the bag and squish the bag to mix the ingredients.

3 Place the ice, the salt, and the bag with the sugar mixture in the quart-sized plastic bag.

Just for
LAUGHS!

WHAT KIND OF PLANE DOESN'T TAKE OFF?
An inclined plane.

4 Wrap the bag in a sheet of newspaper. Then place the wrapped bag in the coffee can and put the lid on the can.

5 Set up an inclined plane with the board against a stack of books or a chair.

6 Roll the can down the inclined plane over and over, until the mixture hardens. This will take about 15 minutes.

7 Open the can and take the bag out. Enjoy your ice cream!

THINGS TO DISCUSS

↑ How did your inclined plane help to mix the ingredients?

↑ Do you think changing the incline or the length of the ramp would have an effect on this activity?

THEN & NOW

Then: Not long ago, people using wheelchairs were unable to enter many public buildings in the United States, because the buildings did not provide ramps.

Now: In 1990, a new law was passed. It said that all new construction in the United States must include a wheelchair ramp or easy access. This law is called the Americans with Disabilities Act.

MINI PUTT GOLF CHALLENGE

SUPPLIES

→ large cardboard box

→ scissors

→ stack of textbooks

→ masking tape

→ plastic cup

→ plastic toy golf putter

→ plastic golf ball

Try the following activity to learn how inclined planes play an important role in creating a golf course.

1 Cut out two large rectangles from the cardboard box. These will be your inclined planes. The measurements are up to you.

2 Place the first inclined plane at a low angle by propping it up with a textbook at one end.

3 Join the second inclined plane to the first with masking tape at the top of the slope. Prop it up with textbooks so that it is higher than the first slope.

4 Place the cup on the floor right behind the highest slope. This will be your hole.

5 Take the mini putter and ball. Stand back a few feet from the first inclined plane. Try to get your ball up the first and second slopes and into the cup. You may need to adjust the angle of your slopes.

VARIATION

↑ Add more elements such as obstacles, a tunnel, or more inclined planes. Can you use inclined planes to make a banked turn?

MAKE YOUR OWN SKI SLOPE

In an Olympic downhill race, athletes try to ski as fast as possible on snow-covered slopes. You can create your own ski slope and racer. Try this activity to learn how fast your racer can go.

1 Arrange your popsicle sticks lengthwise next to each other and tape them together. Draw a figure on heavy paper to ride on the skis, or cut one out from the cover of a magazine. Tape it to the skis so that it is upright.

2 Place the tray on a book to create an angle. Set the skier at the top of the tray.

3 Let go of the skier and time how long it takes it to reach the floor. Write this time down in your journal.

4 Make the inclined plane steeper by adding one book at a time and repeating the experiment. Write down your results in your journal.

5 Try adding more weight to the skis and see if this changes your results.

THINGS TO DISCUSS

↑ How many books did it take to make the skier move at its fastest?

↑ Why were the times different?

WHEELS AND AXLES

A WHEEL AND AN AXLE ARE TWO OBJECTS JOINED TOGETHER AT THEIR CENTER. WHEN ONE ROTATES, THE OTHER DOES TOO.

It's fun to think about what life was like in the past. But can you imagine living before wheels and axles were invented? You wouldn't be able to ride a bike. And you wouldn't be taking the bus to school either.

Wheels and axles come in lots of shapes and sizes. Vehicle wheels, doorknobs, faucet handles, screwdrivers, and airplane propellers are just a few examples. Sometimes a handle called a **crank** is used to get the wheel moving, like the pedal on your bicycle.

WHEELS AND AXLES

No one knows exactly who invented the wheel or when it was invented. One of the earliest known images of a wheel was found on stone carvings from 3500 BCE, which were discovered in Sumer, **Mesopotamia**. The use of wheels spread rapidly throughout Egypt, Europe, and Asia.

How did people move a heavy load before the wheel was invented? They simply had to drag it along the ground! They made the work a little easier by placing a load on a sled and dragging it. Then the idea of pulling a sled over log rollers led to the invention of the **sledge**.

Although the sledge system worked well, it was slow. Imagine constantly moving the back rollers to the front of the sledge to keep things moving. After a lot of use, the heavy loads made grooves in the rollers. These grooves made it easier to move the sledge a greater distance because the sled didn't slide around on top. Over time, the grooves may have acted as axles connecting the wheels.

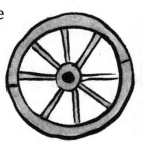

The first wheels didn't look anything like the wheels we have today. They were solid and made entirely of wood. Wheels with **spokes** weren't developed until 2000 BCE. Spoked wheels were faster and lighter compared to solid wheels. One of the first uses of spoked wheels was on Egyptian chariots.

How do we know so much about the history of the wheel? No one has ever travelled back in time except in movies and books. So how do we know so much about how people lived? Because scientists called archaeologists have studied the art, tools, and housing of people from long ago.

spokes: bars or wire rods connecting the center of a wheel to the outside rim.

Tutankhamen: a king who ruled Egypt from 1334 to 1325 BCE.

Archaeologists use information from many sources, including cave paintings, historical records, and burial sites. Kings and other important people were often buried with objects they thought they might need in the next world. For example, **Tutankhamen** was buried with six wooden chariots.

Wheels actually belong to the lever family. A lever that moves all the way around in a circle is called an axle. The center of an axle is the point where the fulcrum used to be.

words 2 know

artifact: an ancient, manmade object.

radiocarbon dating: a scientific test used to date artifacts.

carbon: the building block of most living things, including plants, as well as diamonds, charcoal, and graphite.

Archaeologists can also run tests to learn when **artifacts** were made. **Radiocarbon dating** is one such test. The idea behind this test is that all life forms, including wood, contain **carbon**. When life forms die, they stop taking in new carbon. So by studying the carbon in an artifact, scientists can determine approximately when that artifact was alive. In 2002, for example, a wooden wheel was discovered in the marshes of Slovenia in Europe. Radiocarbon dating put the wheel at 3000 BCE. This made it the oldest wooden wheel ever discovered.

WHEEL INVENTIONS

The wheel is one of the most important inventions in human history. We usually think of the wheel as a tool that makes transportation easier. But there are lots of other uses of the wheel that have been around for a very long time.

POTTERY WHEEL: A pottery wheel lies flat, like a plate. As it spins around an axle, the wheel allows a potter to shape wet clay without moving around. The invention of the pottery wheel made the process of making pottery faster. Before its invention, people mostly made things out of clay only to use in their own homes. With the pottery wheel, people could make a lot of pottery and earn money by selling it. Early pottery wheels date back to 3500 BCE, even before the use of wheels in transportation.

THEN & NOW

Then: Long ago, an assistant turned the pottery wheel by hand while the potter shaped the clay.

Now: Today, most pottery wheels are powered by electric motors.

WATER WHEEL: The water wheel is a large wheel with blades or buckets made of wood or metal. When placed in fast-flowing water, the wheel is pushed around and around. It produces power that can move equipment, such as large grinding stones in mills. Water wheels were also placed under falling water that filled the buckets or pushed the paddles to spin the wheel. The history of the water wheel goes back to around 100 BCE.

ASTROLABE: The astrolabe is a disc with a rotating arm that measures the position of the stars. In Greek it means "star-finder." The astrolabe is thought to have been created by the Greek astronomer Hipparchus around 150 BCE. This instrument can determine the hours of the day and the positions of the sun, moon, and stars. Centuries later, explorers such as Samuel de Champlain relied on the astrolabe while sailing through unknown North American waters.

BICYCLE: The first bicycle was invented by Comte De Sivrac in the 1790s. He called it a celerifere. It didn't have pedals or handlebars. The entire bicycle, including the wheels, was made from wood. It worked like a scooter but you couldn't steer it. Riders had to lift the wheel and point it in the direction they wanted to go. Good riders could steer the bike by doing a "wheelie" to pop up the front tire and shift its direction. Around 20 years later, Karl Drais improved the celerifere by adding a steering wheel. He called his creation a Draisienne and you pushed it with your feet.

Sometimes researchers discover early simple machines in unusual places. The first evidence of a wheelbarrow in Europe was found in a stained glass window in Chartres Cathedral, France. It dates back to 1220 CE.

FERRIS WHEEL: In 1893, the organizers of the Chicago World's Fair wanted something that would amaze the country. Inventor George Washington Gale Ferris, Jr. provided it. It was a massive rotating wheel with 36 cars, 250 feet high (76 meters). Today's Ferris wheels dwarf his original creation. The London Eye in England is the tallest Ferris wheel in Europe at 443 feet tall (135 meters). But the Singapore Flyer tops it at 541 feet (165 meters)!

 **? DID YOU KNOW** The invention of the wheelbarrow is thought to date back to around 100 BCE. Ancient Chinese writings refer to a "wooden ox with handles." Chinese armies used the wheelbarrow to move supplies and injured soldiers.

GEAR WHEELS

Gears are wheels with teeth around the outside. Gear wheels always work in pairs, and the teeth of one wheel fit perfectly into the teeth of the other wheel. When one gear wheel moves, it passes along its motion and force to the second gear. It's like a never-ending game of hot potato!

Depending on how gears are combined, they can control how fast or slow an object moves. When you switch gears on your bicycle it changes how hard or easy it is to pedal. Bicycle gears make it easier for you to climb up a hill or zoom down.

REINVENTING THE WHEEL

Have you ever had a flat tire on your bike? This may not happen in the future. The Michelin tire company has created a tire that does not need air! It's called a Tweel. The Tweel's hub is joined to flexible spokes. The spokes are just as good at absorbing the shocks from the road as air.

An armored vehicle with Tweels can roll over a landmine and keep going. A Tweel is even being developed for Lunar Rovers to drive on the surface of the moon. Tweels aren't quite ready to be used on bikes or cars yet, but they might be by the time you get your license!

MOVING WITH ROLLERS

The Egyptians used rollers to move heavy stone blocks up ramps when building the pyramids. Rollers made their job easier by reducing friction. Pyramid builders pulled on strong ropes that were attached to the blocks. When the roller in back was free, it was moved to the front. It might help to do this with a partner so one can pull and the other can move the rollers.

SUPPLIES

→ plastic laundry basket

→ 10 to 12 books

→ 8 to 10 metal rods or garden stakes

→ journal

1 Place the books in the laundry basket and try to push the basket of books across the floor. Write your observations down in your journal.

2 Now, evenly space the rods out on the floor and place the basket of books on top of the rods.

3 Push the basket of books across the floor using the rollers. You will need to keep moving the last roller to the front. Write your observations down in your journal.

THINGS TO DISCUSS

↑ Was it easier or more difficult to move the basket of books with the rollers?

↑ What force did you use to move the basket across the floor?

WORKING TOGETHER

SUPPLIES

→ peeled raw potato

→ knife

→ toothpicks

→ 3 paper fasteners

→ shoebox lid

→ pen

→ journal

When several gears are put together, they form a gear train. In this activity you'll make large and small gears out of potatoes. You need an adult to help with the knife and the toothpicks.

1 Slice the potato to cut two large wheels and one smaller wheel. The larger wheels should be about 3½ inches across (9 centimeters).

2 Push an equal number of toothpicks into the outside edge of the two large slices, spacing them at regular intervals.

3 Push paper fasteners through the centers of each wheel. Use the paper fasteners to secure the two large slices to the top of the shoebox lid so the toothpicks interlock.

4 Gently turn each gear and watch what happens. Write your observations in your journal.

5 Push half the amount of toothpicks into the outside edge of the smaller wheel.

6 Take one of the large wheels off the box and replace it with the smaller potato wheel, again with the toothpicks interlocking.

7 With a pen, mark one place on the gears where they touch. Turn the gears and see how many times the smaller gear rotates for a single rotation of the larger wheel. Write your observations in your journal.

WHAT'S HAPPENING?

↑ Gears do different jobs depending on their size and how they are grouped. A large gear turning a smaller gear produces more speed. A small gear turning a larger gear produces more power.

THINGS TO DISCUSS

↑ How do the teeth on the potato wheels work together?

↑ In what direction do the gears spin?

↑ How many times does the smaller gear turn compared to the larger gear?

Try This

Did you know that a rolling pin is a wheel and axle? The handles are the axle and the cylinder that rolls out the dough is the wheel.

Try this easy experiment with dough and a rolling pin to find out how a wheel and axle can make work easier.

Take one half of your dough and press it flat using only your hands. Now take the other half and roll it flat with the rolling pin. Was it easier to flatten the dough with a wheel and axle? Can you name some other kitchen tools that have a wheel and axle?

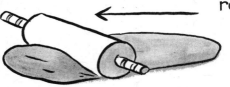

MAKE YOUR OWN
SPINNING TOP

SUPPLIES

- → 2 colors of origami paper
- → ruler
- → pencil
- → scissors
- → toothpick
- → modeling clay

A spinning top is one of the world's oldest toys. It's also an example of a wheel and axle. When the axle is turned, the top spins.

1 Measure a rectangle on each paper, 3 by 1 inches (7 by 2½ centimeters). Cut out the two rectangles.

2 Take one rectangle and fold the corner to the opposite edge to create a triangle. Do the same at the bottom. The square in the center should be about 1 inch (2½ centimeters). Repeat for the other rectangle.

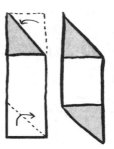

3 Center the squares by placing one rectangle sheet across the other. Fold all of the corners into the middle of the square. Secure the last fold by tucking it inside.

4 Poke a small hole in the center of your square. Insert the toothpick. The square should be closer to one end of the toothpick than the other.

5 Add a small piece of clay to the end of the toothpick closest to the square. Stand the pointy end on a table, hold the top by the clay and give it a spin. It may take a few tries—don't give up!

MAKE YOUR OWN
FRUIT TOP

In rural areas of Indonesia, children craft toy cars out of the rinds of pomelos, a citrus fruit that is like a big grapefruit. Try the following activity to learn why cars wouldn't be able to move without the wheel and axle.

SUPPLIES

→ pomelo or grapefruit

→ knife

→ 2 toothpicks or bamboo skewers

→ thin straw or plastic coffee stirrer

→ string

1 With an adult's help, cut the fruit in half and carefully peel off the skin.

2 Have an adult slice one section of the skin in half again. Put one section aside and cut off the ends of the other to make a rectangle. This will be the body and roof of the car.

3 With the larger section on the bottom, connect it to the rectangular roof with toothpicks or bamboo skewers.

4 Cut out two circles for wheels from the other half of the skin.

5 Put a straw through the body of the car and attach a wheel on each side.

6 Poke a small hole through the tip of one end of the car and tie a string through it to pull your car along.

SCREWS

A SCREW IS AN INCLINED PLANE WRAPPED AROUND A SHAFT. IT ALLOWS THE SCREW TO MOVE IN A CIRCULAR PATTERN AND PULLS ONE THING TOWARD ANOTHER.

We all know what screws are. They look like nails with grooves in them. It's amazing all the places where screws are used. You turn screws to keep instruments in tune, to tighten a clamp, and to put in light bulbs. Some types of screws are even used in surgery.

Unlike a nail, which has a flat head, a screw has a notch in the top. A screwdriver fits into this notch. By turning the screwdriver you tighten the screw.

SCREWS

The grooves of a screw are called **threads**. The distance between the threads is called the **pitch**. Threads wind evenly around the body of a screw—sort of like a winding slide on a playground.

1, 2, 3, 4, 5,

6, 7, 8, 9 . . .

Because of the threads, screws hold on tightly and cannot easily be pulled out. When a screw's threads are closer together, it takes more turns to tighten it. If you want to know how many turns it will take to twist the screw all the way in, just count the threads!

THE ROBERTSON SCREW

In 1908, Peter Lymburner Robertson created a screw with a very deep square opening on the head. He also **designed** a screwdriver with a square end to fit securely in his new screw. Because the screwdriver didn't slip out, you could use the screwdriver with one hand. This helped people work faster. Soon, big companies like the Ford Motor Company were using his design. The Model T car made by Ford used over 700 Robertson screws! These screws are still popular in Canada today.

TYPES OF SCREWS

Screws are important. They're used in submarine hatches so water doesn't get in. Ice climbers use long metal screws to help them climb. But to discover the benefit of screws, just look around your kitchen. Corkscrews, jar lids, bottle caps, and spinning stools are all examples of screws.

words 2 know

bolt: a strong screw used with a nut to fasten things.

worm gear: a rod with threads that fits against another gear.

spur gear: a disc with teeth that fits into another gear.

BOLT: The strongest type of screw is a **bolt**. Unlike other screws, a bolt does not cut into the material being fastened. Instead, it goes through a hole in the material and is then held in place by a nut on the other end. Both the bolt and the nut have threads, just like a regular screw, so they fit tightly together. Bolts are used to join machinery and furniture.

WORM GEAR: A **worm gear** looks like a screw. Its threads are fitted against a toothed wheel called a **spur gear**. Stringed instruments use tuning screws to keep them in tune. A tuning screw is made of a knob and a worm gear. When the musician turns the knob, the gears move, tightening the string. The use of worm gears to tune instruments dates to the sixteenth century.

SCREWS

drill bit: a tool used in a drill to cut material.

DRILL BIT: Have you ever seen one of your parents use an electric drill at home? The drill holds a cutting tool called a **drill bit**, which spins very fast. Drill bits cut holes into wood, metal, stone, and plastic. The drill bit is pointed at one end and its edges have threads just like a screw. As the drill bit turns, pieces of material like wood or metal are pulled up the threads and out.

Drill bits come in different shapes and sizes depending on the job they have to perform. The largest drill bit in the world is the size of a train! It was used to make a subway tunnel in Germany and a train tunnel through the Swiss Alps.

HOW SCREWS CAN LIFT

The jackscrew is a simple machine used to lift and support heavy things like a piece of machinery or even a house! The jack has a strong screw that comes out of a base at the bottom. The jack goes under the object being lifted and at the top of the screw is a surface to support the weight. The most common type of jackscrew is a car jack. This is what your parents might use to lift their car to fix a flat tire.

Just for LAUGHS!

WHAT TYPE OF THREAD CAN'T BE USED FOR SEWING?
A screw thread.

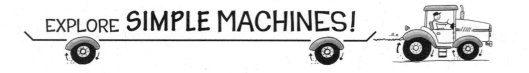

How does a jackscrew work? With help from another simple machine—the lever. First, a metal bar is inserted into the jack. The bar is turned clockwise. This turning makes the screw rise out of the base. Whatever is resting on top of the jack is pushed upwards.

Many years ago, jackscrews were used to raise elevators. In 1853, Elisha Graves Otis invented the first jackscrew elevator, which was equipped with an automatic safety system. Before this, elevators were lifted with pulleys—that sometimes snapped! Jackscrew elevators were safer, but they wore out quickly due to friction. They also moved at a snail's pace of 6 feet per minute (2 meters). Today, you can take an electric elevator to the top of the Empire State Building at a speed of 1,400 feet per minute (426 meters). That's a lot faster than climbing the 1,860 stairs to the top!

? DID YOU KNOW An American artist named Andrew Meyers makes portraits entirely out of screws. He drills in 7,000 to 10,000 screws at different depths to make 3D images of peoples' faces. After all the screws are in, he paints over the face to make it look like a portrait and not a screw sculpture.

HISTORY OF THE SCREW

The history of the screw begins with our old friend Archimedes, the Greek scientist who was the first person to understand how levers worked. Around 250 BCE, Archimedes created one of the first recorded screw machines. But his machine didn't hold things together. It was used to pump water!

Archimedes' machine was a large screw inside a hollow tube. A person placed one end of the tube into water, then turned a crank. The crank caused the screw to turn, and the water at the bottom was brought up the tube along the turning spiral. Compared to hoisting up buckets of water by hand, the Archimedes screw moved water with a lot less work!

HANGING GARDENS OF BABYLON

The most famous gardens in history were the Hanging Gardens of Babylon, near present-day Iraq. It is believed that the gardens were built around 600 BCE by King Nebuchadnezzar II for his wife. The gardens were one of the Seven Wonders of the Ancient World. There are no ruins of the gardens and today many people wonder if they ever really existed.

Archaeologists believe the Hanging Gardens probably did not hang, but were terraced, like steps. Water from the Euphrates River kept the gardens green. It is not known what method was used to pump the water. Some scholars believe a screw pump might have been used, but the Archimedes water screw was not built until later.

Today, there are new ways to pump water, but the Archimedes screw is still being used in many places. For example, SeaWorld Adventure Park in San Diego uses two Archimedes screws to lift water for one of their rides.

In 1440, a German printer and publisher named Johannes Gutenberg used screws for his printing press. This is one of the most important inventions in modern history. Printed books could be created more quickly than handwritten ones. The printing press worked by turning a large screw with a handle, forcing down a plate. The plate then pressed a sheet of paper onto a tray with inked metal letters, or type.

Screws aren't used only for work, but for play too! Since 400 CE, kids in China have been playing with a flying toy that moved like a helicopter. It was made of wood with leather straps tied to the blades. This flying toy was a propeller on a stick. Eventually these toys made their way to Europe. Today, they are sold as puddle jumpers or whirligigs.

Just for LAUGHS!

WHAT LOOKS LIKE A WINDING ROAD BUT YOU CANNOT DRIVE ON IT?

A screw!

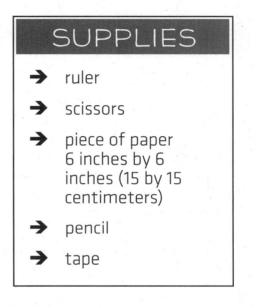

MAKE YOUR OWN
SCREW

When an inclined plane is wrapped around a rod, it becomes a screw. Try this activity to make your own screw with just a pencil and paper.

1 Fold the paper in half so that it forms a triangle. Cut along the fold. Draw a line along the longest edge of the triangle.

2 Turn the paper over so the side with the line faces down. Lay your pencil down on one of the short sides of the triangle.

3 Tape the edge of the triangle to the pencil. Wrap the paper triangle around the pen tightly and tape it in place.

THINGS TO DISCUSS

↑ What does the pencil line look like now?

↑ Why do you think the paper spirals?

↑ How is this object like a screw?

THEN & NOW

Then: In ancient times, Archimedes screw pumps lifted water from low-lying rivers or canals.

Now: Archimedes screws the size of pencil erasers are used to keep blood pumping during heart surgery.

MAKE YOUR OWN JACK

SUPPLIES

➔ 2 plastic lids

➔ scissors

➔ 3-inch bolt and nut (7 centimeters)

➔ tape

➔ journal

Did you know that screws can be used to lift heavy objects? While small jacks can only lift the corner of a car, larger screw jacks can lift an entire vehicle. Have an adult help you with the scissors.

1 Using the scissors, take one of the plastic lids and make a hole in the middle. It should be slightly larger than the diameter of the bolt.

2 Insert the bolt into the hole from the underside of the lid and secure with tape. This piece should be able to stand on a flat surface.

3 Make a hole in the middle of the second lid. This lid will face up to form your platform. Place the nut under the hole and secure with tape. Do not put tape over the center.

4 Place the bottom lid (with the bolt) on a flat surface and twist the nut in the second lid counterclockwise onto the bolt. Record you observations in your journal. Now twist the nut clockwise. What happens?

THINGS TO DISCUSS

↑ Do you need to apply gentle force or strong force to turn the screw?

↑ Where would this type of machine be helpful?

LET'S DO THE TWIST

Most machines need screws to hold them together. Try this activity to discover why screws are a stronger fastener than nails.

1 Using the hammer, pound the nail into the block of wood.

2 Now use the screwdriver to insert the screw into the block.

3 Remove the nail from the wood using the end of the hammer.

4 Now try to remove the screw from the wood using the end of the hammer.

SUPPLIES

→ hammer

→ nail

→ block of wood

→ screwdriver

→ screw

→ journal

5 Record your discoveries in your journal.

WHAT'S HAPPENING?

↑ Friction holds the nail and screw in place. The screw's threads allow it to resist friction better. It grips the wood. While a nail can be pulled directly out of the wood, a screw must be turned. This is why there is an advantage to using screws instead of nails to hold things together.

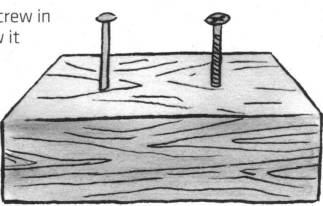

MAKE YOUR OWN HELICOPTER

SUPPLIES

→ pencil
→ ruler
→ scissors
→ paper clip

It is easy to make a flying machine out of paper. Try this activity to learn how helicopter blades act like a screw.

1 Measure and cut out a strip of paper 5 inches long and ½ inch wide (10 by 1 centimeter).

2 Fold the paper in half and put a paperclip on the folded edge. Only insert it three-quarters of the way.

3 Fold the top wings down at an angle. They should stick out slightly.

4 Hold the helicopter by the paper clip. Stand on a chair or at the top of a staircase and drop it.

THINGS TO DISCUSS

↑ Which way does the helicopter spin, clockwise or counterclockwise?

↑ What happens if the wings are more or less at an angle?

WOW!!

Leonardo da Vinci designed a helicopter more than 500 years before the first one was built. He sketched a flying machine that resembled today's helicopter and called it the Helical Air Screw. Inspired by this drawing, Igor I. Sikorsky designed the first working helicopter in the late 1930s.

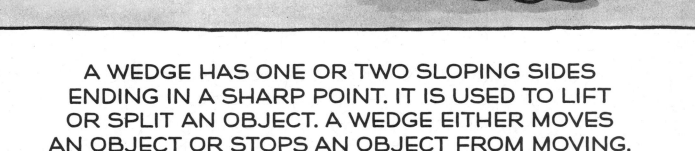

WEDGES

A WEDGE HAS ONE OR TWO SLOPING SIDES ENDING IN A SHARP POINT. IT IS USED TO LIFT OR SPLIT AN OBJECT. A WEDGE EITHER MOVES AN OBJECT OR STOPS AN OBJECT FROM MOVING.

You don't slice apples with a spoon, do you? You use a knife, which is a simple machine called a wedge. Wedges do more than just cut—they push apart, divide, and split objects. Wedges work when you put a narrow end into something you want to come apart, and apply force to the wider end. For example, you slice an apple by pushing down on a knife. The knife takes your downward force and turns it into a sideways force. Cool!

A doorstop is an example of a single wedge. It has one sloping side. Single wedges are placed flat on the ground, mostly used to stop things from moving.

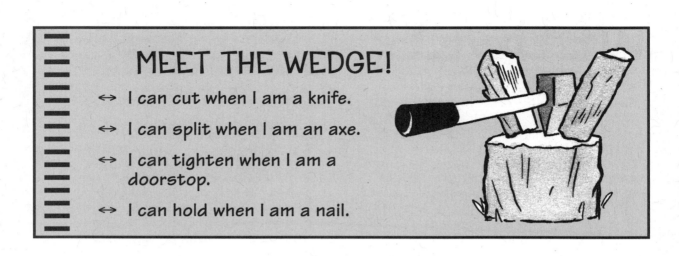

MEET THE WEDGE!

↔ I can cut when I am a knife.

↔ I can split when I am an axe.

↔ I can tighten when I am a doorstop.

↔ I can hold when I am a nail.

Single

Sculptors use a single wedge called a chisel to shape ice, wood, and stone. They push the thinner end of the chisel into the material they wish to shape. Tapping on the opposite end of the chisel with a mallet causes the excess material to separate. In this way, sculptors create fantastic shapes.

Double

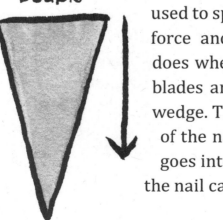

Double wedges have two sloping sides and are used to split, fasten, or cut. They take a downward force and push this force outwards like an axe does when it splits a log. Knives, shovels, and razor blades are all double wedges. A nail is also a double wedge. The point makes an opening for the wider part of the nail to enter. When the wider body of the nail goes into the opening, it pushes apart the material so the nail can get all the way through.

WEDGE HISTORY

No one knows who invented the wedge. Some wedges, like claws or teeth, are natural. Nobody "made them." But tools were first made by humans millions of years ago. Instead of simply using a stick or a stone, humans began to alter them. For example, they took a hard stone and used it to hammer a softer stone. Hammering away at the sides of the softer stone created sharp edges, and in this way a wedge-shaped tool took form. Early humans also made wedges out of wood, bone, and shell.

These wedges were used for cutting, scraping, splitting, and digging. They were also used as weapons. Wedges were attached to the end of sticks to make spears and arrowheads. Wedges were used for hunting. With stone knives, **Paleolithic** hunters killed large animals like mastodons or the woolly mammoth. Once the animal was killed, the wedge could be used for cutting and scraping the meat from the skin.

Coastal tribes in North America used wedges to hunt as well, but they put a different spin on it. First they built long fences in the shape of a wedge. Then hunters would frighten deer into the enclosure—which gradually narrowed. As the deer tried to exit the wedge, they could be speared.

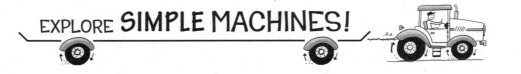

Other tribes used wedges to dig and farm. For example, a digging stick had a wedge-shaped bottom that was hardened by fire. Digging sticks made it easier to separate soil, to dig up roots, or to plant seeds.

WEDGES IN CONSTRUCTION

In an earlier chapter, you learned that the Great Pyramid of Giza contains over 2 million stone blocks. Ancient Egyptians used wedges to dig and shape these giant blocks. First they chipped away at the stone with a chisel until wooden wedges could be inserted in natural cracks in the stone. The wedges were soaked in water to make them swell. This made it easier to split the stone.

words (2) know

ravine: a deep river valley carved by running water.

The Romans were famous for their use of wedges in construction. They built wonderful stone arches with them. Many of these arches held up impressive bridges, some of which still stand today. For example, the Tagus Bridge, built in Spain in 105 CE, spans an entire **ravine**. Romans built the Tagus Bridge using wedge-shaped stone blocks. The blocks were cut to fit together perfectly into a sturdy semi-circle arch. The block at the top of the arch was called the keystone. That's because it was the key to holding the bridge up!

caravan: a group of traders who travelled together.

UNESCO World Heritage Site: a special place named by UNESCO that deserves to be protected for future generations. UNESCO stands for United Nations Educational, Scientific and Cultural Organization.

A CARVED CITY!

Most cities are constructed piece by piece. But the famous ancient city of Petra was actually carved straight out of a mountain! Nearly all of its hundreds of temples and tombs were cut directly out of pink sandstone with wedge-shaped hand tools.

Located in Jordan, Petra was built by the Nabataeans, an Arab tribe who settled the area sometime around 250 BCE. They were known for their trading, agricultural, and stone-carving skills. At one time, about 20,000 people lived in Petra and it was an important stop on the **caravan** routes of the Middle East. Today, the ancient city is a **UNESCO World Heritage Site** visited by thousands of tourists each year.

According to the Guinness Book of World Records, the narrowest house in the world is in Scotland. Built in 1875, the house is shaped like a piece of cheese and is nicknamed "The Wedge." The front of the house, which is the narrowest point, is only 4 feet wide (1¼ meters). That's just enough room for a front door. Talk about a tight squeeze!

WOW!!

FARMING WITH WEDGES

For thousands of years, farmers worked the land with a type of wedge called a plow. Farm animals pulled the plow. It loosened the soil so seeds could be planted more easily. John Deere was a pioneer and inventor from Vermont. In 1837, Deere invented the steel walking plow. He made it from the steel of a broken saw blade. The strong blade made it possible for farmers to plow the dense soil of North America's Midwest. Deere sold his plow across America. Today his company still sells farm equipment.

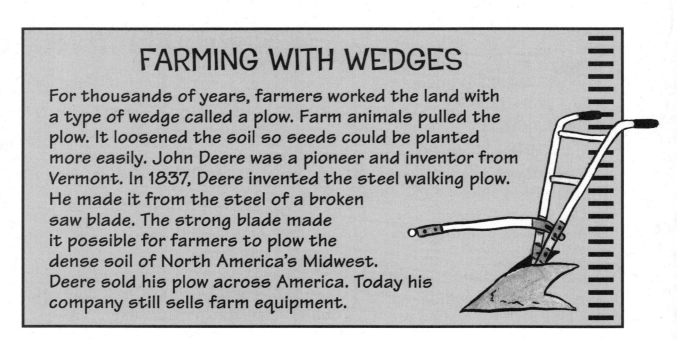

WEDGES TODAY

Today, wedges are used for many different jobs. Spatulas are wedges that help get hot pizzas out of the oven. Razor blades are wedges that get rid of unwanted hair. And on the golf course, players use sand wedges to get out of sand traps. Even the zipper on your coat uses wedges. The zipper has wedges on either side of the slider. They line the teeth up and push them together. When the slider is pulled down, the wedges pull the teeth apart. Try it out and see for yourself!

Just for **LAUGHS!**

WHAT DID THE COAT SAY TO THE ZIPPER?
Loosen up!

EXPERIMENTING WITH WEDGES

Smile wide and say "cheese." You just showed your wedges! Teeth are wedges. In the next activity, find out which teeth are used to bite food and which are used to chew food, and why.

SUPPLIES

→ peach
→ apple
→ bread roll
→ journal

1 Wash and dry the peach and apple. Set the fruit to one side.

2 Take a bite of the peach, noting which teeth you used.

3 Take a bite of the apple and note which teeth you used.

4 Take a bite of the bread and note which teeth you used.

5 Now bite the food again, chew it, and note which teeth you used for chewing. Record your results in your journal.

WHAT'S HAPPENING?

↑ Your teeth help to break down food into smaller pieces. The teeth in the front of your mouth look like narrow wedges. Narrow wedges cut more easily than wider wedges. The teeth at the back of your mouth called molars, are short and wide. They look like wide wedges. Wide wedges grind up food.

CHOMP

MAKE YOUR OWN BOAT

SUPPLIES

→ 59-ounce juice carton (1¾ liters)

→ ruler

→ pencil

→ scissors

→ masking tape

→ waterproof markers

→ popsicle sticks

→ clay

→ tub of water

→ string

→ journal

The front of a boat is shaped like a wedge. This design helps the boat slice through the water. Try the next activity to find out what would happen if the front of a boat was square. Have an adult help with the scissors.

1 Place the carton sideways on a table. Make sure the opening is face up.

2 Use a ruler and a pencil to mark the halfway point (lengthwise) on the container. Cut the container in half. This is the boat's hull, or body.

3 Cover the entire hull of your boat with masking tape. Use the markers to create a design on the hull. You can even give your boat a name!

4 Lie the popsicle sticks across the hull to create seats. Hold the sticks in place with clay.

5 Try floating your boat in a tub full of water.

6 Next attach a piece of string to the pointy front (bow) of the boat, with tape. Pull the boat through the water.

7 Take the string off the bow and attach it to the back of the boat (called the stern). Pull the boat through the water. Record your results in your journal.

Just for LAUGHS!

WHAT DiD THE APPLE SAY TO THE WEDGE?
You split me up!

THINGS TO DISCUSS

↑ Was it easier to pull the boat from the front or from the back?

↑ How did the water move when the boat was pulled by the front compared to the back?

↑ What else did you notice?

Try This

Get two sheets of paper, some yarn, a needle, and a stir stick. Thread the needle with yarn and make five stitches through the paper. Knot another piece of yarn onto a stir stick. Now try sewing through the paper using the stir stick. Compare the pieces of paper and write down your observations.

Unlike the stir stick, the needle is a wedge. Its sharp point, formed by two inclined planes, makes it easier to sew with. That's why it takes less effort to push the needle through the paper. It's also why the paper doesn't tear.

LET'S CARVE FRUIT

SUPPLIES

→ banana
→ cutting board
→ small knife
→ plate
→ kiwi
→ raisins

A knife is a simple machine that allows you to slice through food. In this activity, it will help you turn a simple banana into a dolphin. Be sure to ask an adult for help with the knife. Wash your hands before you begin.

1 Peel the banana and place it on the cutting board so the curves of the banana face up.

2 Slice the bottom off the banana so it can rest on a flat surface. Keep this slice. Put the banana on the plate.

3 Use the knife to cut out a wedge on the front for the dolphin's mouth. Keep the wedge you cut out.

THEN & NOW

Then: To clear a road after a snowstorm, horses dragged wooden wedge plows through the snow.

Now: Snowplows are equipped with large metal wedges on the front. These wedges push the snow to the side of the road to clear a path for cars.

4 Make a slit in the top toward the front of the dolphin and insert the mouth wedge to make a top fin.

5 Make a slit at the tail end and insert the slice you cut from the belly. This will be the tail fin.

6 Peel the kiwi and cut it into slices ¼ inch thick (½ centimeter). Cut one slice in half for the dorsal fins of the dolphin. You can simply prop these up against the banana. Add raisins on top for the eyes.

7 Arrange the rest of the kiwi around your plate for the waves. Now your banana dolphin is ready to eat. Try creating more creatures with other fruits and vegetables.

BENJAMIN FRANKLIN'S FIN WEDGES

Benjamin Franklin was a printer, librarian, statesman, and inventor. As a boy, he loved to go swimming. At the age of 11, he created wedges, or swim fins, to allow him to move through the water faster. Ben fashioned his swim fins from wood and wore them on his hands and feet.

PULLEYS

PULLEYS ARE GROOVED WHEELS WITH ROPES TO LIFT AND LOWER HEAVY THINGS WITH EASE.

> Do you have a bike at your home? How about a clothesline or window blinds? Your school probably has a flagpole. If so, you've seen and used plenty of pulleys.

The pulley is an amazing tool. That's why you'll find them at schools, construction sites, ski hills, and in your home. Sailors use pulleys to raise heavy sails up the mast. Tow-truck drivers lift cars with pulleys. Cranes that build skyscrapers use pulleys, and so do elevators.

PULLEYS

Like many simple machines, no one knows who invented the pulley. The simplest pulleys may have been made from a rope and a tree branch! A clever person tossed a rope over a branch and tied one end to the object to be lifted.

By using a pulley, we can use all our weight to pull down on the rope. We can even hang on the end of the rope if we have to. That's a lot easier than pulling up on the rope! Pulleys help us by changing the direction of the force we use to lift an object. Instead of pulling up, we pull down.

words 2 know

fixed pulley: the pulley is joined to a point that does not move.

movable pulley: the pulley and the load move together.

compound pulley: when fixed and movable pulleys work together.

PARTS OF A PULLEY

Branches are not a part of pulleys today. We use wheels instead. A rope or chain is placed around the wheel and axle. A deep groove in the wheel keeps the rope in place. The object to be lifted is tied to one end of the rope. When the rope is pulled down, it makes the wheel turn, and the load moves up.

TYPES OF PULLEYS

There are three types of pulleys: a **fixed pulley**, a **movable pulley**, and a **compound pulley**. How the wheel and rope are put together, determines the type of pulley.

69

A fixed pulley does not move. The pulley is attached to a surface like a hook, post, or a wall, to keep it firmly in place. The rope moves but the pulley does not.

The flagpole at your school uses a fixed pulley. The pulley is located at the top and bottom of the pole. It does not move up or down but the flag does. When you pull down on the rope, the pulley raises the flag up the pole. A fixed pulley is helpful for raising an object to a level above your head.

A movable pulley is attached to the load. One end of the rope is attached to a point that does not move. The other end of the rope is left free. When you pull on the rope, the pulley wheel moves, bringing the load with it. The pulley is hung between two portions of rope. Each portion of rope helps support the load, making it easier to lift. This type of pulley is good if you are trying to raise an object below you up to your level.

THEN & NOW

Then: Pulleys relied on people power, water wheels, and steam engines to make them turn.

Now: Pulley systems in modern machinery, like cranes, rely on motorized engines.

PULLEYS

A zip line is a movable pulley system that moves objects or people from one place to another. They allow people to fly above rivers and forest canopies safely. A zip line's steel cable stretches between two fixed points. The rider is harnessed to the pulley. When riders push off from a platform, they ride along with the pulley, propelled by gravity.

COMPOUND PULLEYS

When fixed and movable pulleys work together, it's a compound pulley. Compound pulleys allow a person to lift objects up and double the strength of his or her force at the same time. Tower cranes at construction sites use compound pulleys. Strong cables and pulleys allow cranes to lift steel and concrete hundreds of feet in the air.

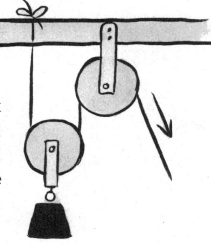

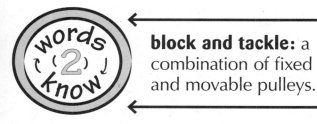

block and tackle: a combination of fixed and movable pulleys.

A **block and tackle** is one type of compound pulley used to lift very heavy objects. It uses both fixed pulleys and movable pulleys that are free to go up and down. A long rope or cable is looped around the pulleys to lift the heavy load. Sailors use this type of pulley to raise and lower sails on ships.

WOW!!

Most people in New York City take the subway to work, but some people take an aerial tram. Passengers travel in cars hanging as high as 250 feet above the ground on cables running through motorized pulleys. Now that's a strong zip line!

Remember the Greek scientist Archimedes? By this time, you probably won't be surprised to learn that Archimedes is thought to have created the first block and tackle pulley system.

When the Greek city of Syracuse was under attack from the Romans, Archimedes created the "ship shaker." This was a giant claw with a crane-like arm that had a hook on the end. A block and tackle pulley system controlled the claw.

The hook was dangled over the city's walls into the harbor. When an enemy ship entered the harbor, the hook was lowered to grab the front of the ship, and lifted high into the air. When the ship was dropped hard back into the sea, it soon sank. The ship shaker is also known as "The Claw of Archimedes."

THAT'S MEDIEVAL!

You don't have to travel back in time to experience the past. In France, workers are building a castle right now with tools and materials used in the **Middle Ages**. No electricity, modern cranes, or bulldozers. Instead, workers use simple machines like rope pulleys to lift loads. The castle, called Chateau de Guedelon, should be completed sometime in the 2020s. It will be a true copy of a **medieval** castle.

PULLEYS IN HISTORY

The ancient Greeks also invented the crane. Without it, they would never have been able to build large buildings like the Parthenon. The Romans improved upon the crane design by using a three-pulley system and later a massive five-pulley system. It allowed the Romans to lift objects of greater weight. These cranes were powered by people walking along giant tread wheels, which were large versions of hamster wheels. How would you like that job?

words 2 know

Middle Ages: the period of time between the end of the Roman Empire and the Renaissance, about 350 to 1450 CE.

medieval: from the Middle Ages.

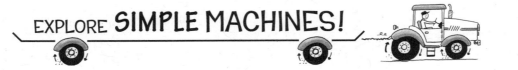

Pulleys were also used to lift elevators in the ancient world. These ancient elevators were operated by human or animal power. Even the Roman Coliseum had elevators! The Coliseum was a huge arena that could hold about 50,000 spectators.

Romans came to watch men fight each other and wild beasts. Wild animals were lifted up to the main fighting level by 28 elevators spread throughout the arena. It took over 200 people, working together on the pulleys, levers, and ropes, to raise all the elevators at once.

windlass: a machine with a rope or chain wrapped around a drum, that is used to lift objects.

 **DID YOU KNOW**

The Abbey of Mont St. Michel, France, is famous for its location at the top of a 262-foot-high rock (82 meters). It also contains the oldest known elevator, built in 1203. A wheeled cart moved up the steep stone ramp of the abbey by pulley and rope. To move the pulley, people or animals walked inside a large, cage-like wheel to turn a cable around a drum called a **windlass**.

MAKE YOUR OWN MOVABLE PULLEY

Try this activity to pick magnets off the floor with help from a movable pulley. Have an adult help with the scissors.

1 Carefully poke a hole 1½ inches (4 centimeters) down each side of your container. Use the scissors.

2 Thread a piece of string through the holes. Tie knots in each end to form a small handle.

3 Tape the magnet to the bottom of the container with clear tape. Set this to one side.

4 Cut a length of string about a yard long (1 meter). Tie one end of the string to a door handle.

5 Loop the other end of the string through the handle of your container.

6 Scatter the paper clips on the floor, directly beneath the doorknob.

7 Try to pick up the paper clips using your movable pulley. Pull on the string to move the load.

SUPPLIES

→ small plastic container
→ scissors
→ string
→ magnet
→ clear tape
→ paper clips

THINGS TO DISCUSS

↑ See how the pulley moves on the string.

↑ When the pulley moves, what does the load do?

SINGLE PULLEY RELAY

SUPPLIES

→ 4 people
→ play structure or tree house
→ 2 ropes
→ 4 pails
→ about 20 golf balls

This fun game will have you and your friends making a fixed single pulley from everyday objects. See which team can move all its golf balls from the bottom of a play structure or tree house to the top first.

1 Make up teams of two people each. Decide which partner will be at the top of the play structure and who will remain at the bottom. You can take turns.

2 Each team gets a rope and two pails. Tie the rope to one of the pails. Then loop the rope over a beam of the play structure.

3 Place the other pail at the top of the structure, to collect the golf balls.

4 Each team gets half the golf balls. Put them in a pile at the bottom of the play structure.

5 Everyone needs to get in position. When both teams are ready, have someone yell go.

WOW!!

What do you need to lift a load that's extremely heavy? An extreme pulley! An example of an extreme pulley is the Taisun, the world's largest crane. Built at a shipyard in China, the Taisun is bigger than a football field and 30 stories high! In 2008, the Taisun set a world record by lifting a barge that weighed over 44 million pounds (almost 20 million kilograms)!

6 The person at the bottom of the pulley will place one golf ball in the pail and pull down on the rope to raise the pail.

7 The player at the top removes the golf ball and places it in the empty pail.

8 The player on the ground then lowers the pail back to the ground.

9 Repeat steps 6 to 8 until one team gets all its golf balls in the empty pail at the top of the structure. The team that does this first, wins.

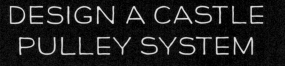

DESIGN A CASTLE PULLEY SYSTEM

SUPPLIES

→ 16-ounce milk or cream container (500 milliliters)

→ scissors

→ ruler

→ pencil

→ yarn

→ tape

→ thin straw

→ colored paper

→ glue

→ markers

To enter a castle, visitors had to cross a drawbridge. Sometimes it spanned a deep moat or ditch. Chains were fitted to the drawbridge and attached to pulleys. This allowed the drawbridge to be raised if the castle was under attack. Have an adult help with the scissors.

1 Cut the back off the carton. In the middle of the front of the carton, draw a rectangle 5 by 6 inches (13 by 15 centimeters). This will be the drawbridge.

2 Carefully cut out the top and sides of your drawbridge. Do not cut along the bottom.

3 Cut two, 15-inch pieces of yarn (38 centimeters).

4 Tape one end of each piece to the top of the drawbridge.

5 About 1 inch (2½ centimeters) above the opening on the carton, poke two holes through the carton and thread the other ends of the yarn pieces through them.

6 On the sides of the container, mark the halfway point between the front and back. The marks should be at the same height as the holes on the front.

7 Make holes at these marks. Push the straw all the way through the holes.

8 Wrap each piece of yarn around the straw once.

9 Now make a hole in the center of the bottom piece of the carton, below the drawbridge.

10 Thread both pieces of yarn through this hole. Tie the two pieces of yarn together with a knot. You have a working pulley.

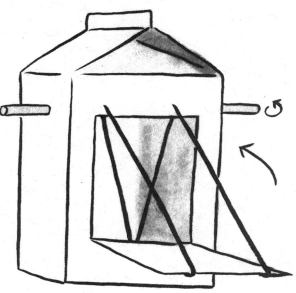

11 Cut paper to fit the sides of your castle and glue it on. Finish decorating it with markers.

12 Use your pulley to raise and lower the drawbridge by twisting the straw.

Just for LAUGHS!

IF ARCHIMEDES HAD PLAYED FOOTBALL, WHAT WOULD HAVE BEEN HIS FAVORITE MOVE?
The block and tackle.

BE AN INVENTOR

Who can become an inventor? You can! Creating something new is exciting. If you have ever tried to design and build an invention then you have already begun. But what is an invention? An invention is any combination of simple machines—the lever, inclined plane, wheel and axle, screw, wedge, and pulley.

But have you ever wondered who invents things? Engineers do. Engineers can be inventors. They are creative people who use math and science to design and build many of the products and structures you see and use every day.

80

BE AN INVENTOR

engineering design process: engineers identify problems and come up with solutions.

construct: putting parts together to make something.

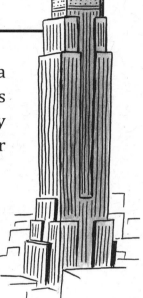

Have you ever seen a skyscraper? How about a spaceship? Maybe you've ridden a bike or take a bus to school. All of these things are made possible by engineers. In fact, nearly everything you see, touch, or feel, was designed by an engineer!

In this chapter you are going to use combinations of simple machines to create a fantastic new machine. Who knows, your design may be used by people in the future.

ENGINEERING DESIGN PROCESS

Many of the projects and activities in this book asked you to look at problems and come up with solutions to those problems. This is what engineers call the **engineering design process**. Here's how the engineering design process works:

- ↔ Identify a problem.
- ↔ Do research.
- ↔ Invent solutions.
- ↔ Choose one solution to test.

- ↔ Design a model.
- ↔ **Construct** the model.
- ↔ Test the model and change it according to the results.

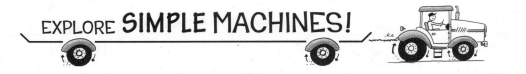
TYPES OF ENGINEERS

Engineering is an exciting career. There are many different types of engineers. You could be a civil, electrical, mechanical, environmental, or aerospace engineer. Which type of engineering appeals to you?

CIVIL: These creative people come up with practical solutions to everyday problems. They have to invent, design, and build structures like bridges, dams, and tunnels. Famous American landmarks like San Francisco's Golden Gate Bridge and Colorado's Hoover Dam were designed by civil engineers.

ELECTRICAL: Electrical systems like the ones in your home or school computer were designed by electrical engineers. Your home's electrical system powers everything from light switches to appliances.

? DID YOU KNOW The word engineer comes from the Latin word *engine*, meaning "a clever invention."

MECHANICAL: Do you like theme park rides? If so, mechanical engineering may be for you. These engineers design and build mechanical systems in rides, aircraft, and automobiles.

BE AN INVENTOR

ENVIRONMENTAL: These engineers are busy working to provide clean water, minimize pollution, and improve the environment. They often work closely with civil engineers to minimize the impact of humans on the environment.

AEROSPACE: This exciting branch of engineering creates machines that fly. From designing airplanes to constructing spacecrafts, aerospace engineers have a job where the sky is the limit!

SIMPLE TASKS WITH COMPLEX MACHINES

Rube Goldberg was a famous cartoonist. He drew cartoons of hilarious inventions with unusual parts such as boots, bathtubs, or canary cages. Unlike regular machines, which make difficult tasks simpler, Rube's machines made simple tasks more difficult.

Every year there are Rube Goldberg competitions in which teams compete to turn a simple task, such as watering a plant, into a never-ending series of pulleys, gears, and levers. One winning team created a 345-step process to squeeze orange juice!

To learn more about Rube Goldberg visit:
pbskids.org/zoom/games/goldburgertogo/realworld.html

DESIGN A NEW INVENTION

SUPPLIES

→ journal
→ pencil
→ boxes
→ straws
→ paper towel rolls
→ popsicle sticks
→ glue
→ paint
→ crayons
→ scissors

Try this activity to design, make, and test a new invention using simple machines. This activity is fun to do alone or in a group.

1 Decide where your machine will be used, such as a kitchen, office, or playground.

2 Decide what task your machine will accomplish.

3 Sketch your design in your journal. Label each simple machine in your design.

4 Now assemble all the materials you will need to build your machine.

5 Construct your invention and test out your design.

6 Take note of what doesn't work, redesign, and test again.

SCAVENGER HUNT

In this scavenger hunt, investigate the simple machines that are in or near your home. The first team to find two examples of each type of simple machine, wins.

1 Determine a time limit, say 15 or 20 minutes.

2 Go to your kitchen, garage, tool shed, family room, etc. Look in each room carefully. When you find a simple machine, take a photo of it.

3 When the time is up, share your examples. Record your results in your journal.

4 Be sure to list each simple machine in its correct group.

THINGS TO DISCUSS

↑ How do the simple machines you discovered make work easier?

↑ What was the easiest simple machine to find?

↑ Which room of your home had the most simple machines? And why do you think this was?

GLOSSARY

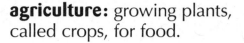

agriculture: growing plants, called crops, for food.

archaeologist: a scientist who studies ancient people through the objects they left behind.

artifact: an ancient, manmade object.

ascent: the way up.

axle: a rod on which a wheel rotates.

BCE: stands for Before the Common Era and counts down to zero.

block and tackle: a combination of fixed and movable pulleys.

bolt: a strong screw used with a nut to fasten things.

caravan: a group of traders who travelled together.

carbon: the building block of most living things, including plants, as well as diamonds, charcoal, and graphite.

catapult: a large war machine used to hurl objects at an enemy.

CE: stands for Common Era and counts up from zero. These are non-religious terms that correspond to BC and AD.

compound machine: two or more simple machines working together.

compound pulley: when fixed and movable pulleys work together.

construct: putting parts together to make something.

counterweight: an object used to balance another object.

crank: a handle that turns a wheel's axle.

defense: protecting against danger.

descent: the way down.

design: to make a sketch or plan, or the way something is made.

drill bit: a tool used in a drill to cut material.

effort: the force that is used on a simple machine to move the load.

engineering design process: engineers identify problems and come up with solutions.

engineer: someone who designs or builds things such as roads, bridges, and buildings.

equilibrium: when forces are balanced.

fixed pulley: the pulley is joined to a point that does not move.

force: a push or a pull.

friction: the force that resists motion between two objects in contact.

GLOSSARY

fulcrum: the point on which a lever turns or pivots.

gravity: a force that pulls all objects to the earth.

inclined plane: a flat surface that connects a lower level to a higher level.

invent: to be the first to think of or make something new.

irrigation ditch: a narrow channel dug in the ground to move water.

lever: a bar that rests on a support and lifts or moves things.

linkage: a link that connects two or more levers together.

load: the object you are moving in your work.

lock: an enclosure in a canal with gates at each end used to raise or lower boats as they pass from one level to another.

lubricant: a substance, like oil or grease, that reduces friction.

mechanical advantage: how a simple machine increases the amount of work someone is able to do. It makes a task easier.

medieval: from the Middle Ages.

Mesopotamia: a region of the Middle East that today is part of Iraq.

Middle Ages: the period of time between the end of the Roman Empire and the Renaissance, about 350 to 1450 CE.

movable pulley: the pulley and the load move together.

Newton: a unit used to measure the amount of force you need to move something.

Paleolithic: the first part of the Stone Age, 750,000 to 15,000 years ago.

pitch: the distance between the threads.

pull: a force that brings something towards you.

pulley: grooved wheels with ropes used to lift something or change its direction.

push: a force that moves something away from you.

radiocarbon dating: a scientific test used to date artifacts.

ravine: a deep river valley carved by running water.

87

GLOSSARY

screw: an inclined plane or lever wrapped around a pole that pulls one thing toward another.

shaduf: an Egyptian device used to raise water.

simple machine: a tool that uses one movement to complete work.

skeleton: a winter sport in which a driver rides head first on a sled.

sledge: a vehicle pulled over rollers.

spokes: bars or wire rods connecting the center of a wheel to the outside rim.

spur gear: a disc with teeth that fits into another gear.

switchback: a road that zigzags back and forth.

thread: a raised edge of a screw that winds around.

trebuchet: a weapon used to throw heavy objects to destroy castles and cities.

Tutankhamen: a king who ruled Egypt from 1334 to 1325 BCE.

unbalanced: when two forces are not equal. This causes motion.

UNESCO World Heritage Site: a special place named by UNESCO that deserves to be protected for future generations. UNESCO stands for United Nations Educational, Scientific and Cultural Organization.

wedge: an object with slanted sides ending in a sharp edge that lifts or splits another object.

weight: a measure of the force of gravity on an object.

wheel and axle: a wheel with a rod that turn together to lift and move loads. The axle is the rod around which the wheel rotates.

windlass: a machine with a rope or chain wrapped around a drum, that is used to lift objects.

work: a force that moves an object a distance.

worm gear: a rod with threads that fits against another gear.

BOOKS

* Anderson, Maxine. *Amazing Leonardo da Vinci Inventions You Can Build Yourself.* Nomad Press, 2006.

* Ardley, Neil. *Science Book of Machines.* Harcourt Brace, 1992.

* Dahl, Michael. *Scoop, Seesaw, and Raise: A Book about Levers.* Picture Window Books, 2003.

* Dahl, Michael. *Twist, Dig, and Drill: A Book about Screws.* Picture Window Books, 2006.

* Glover, David. *Pulleys and Gears.* Heineman Library, 1997.

* Hewitt, Sally. *Machines We Use.* Grolier Publishing, 2005.

* Hodge, Deborah. *Simple Machines.* Kids Can Press, 1998.

* Isogawa, Yoshihito. *The LEGO Technic Idea Book: Simple Machines.* No Starch Press, 2010.

* Macaulay, David. *The New Way Things Work.* Houghton Mifflin Books for Children, 1998.

* Nankivell-Aston, Sally. *Science Experiments With Simple Machines.* Children's Press, 2000.

* Oxlade, Chris. *Levers.* Smart Apple Media, 2008.

* Pulver, Robin. *Axle Annie.* Puffin Books, 2001.

* Solway, Andrew. *Castle Under Siege!: Simple Machines.* Heinemann-Raintree, 2005.

* Tocci, Salvatore. *Experiments With Simple Machines.* Children's Press, 2003.

* Woods, Mary B. *Ancient Machines: From Wedges to Waterwheels.* Runeston Press, 1999.

89

RESOURCES

WEB SITES

Automaton at Gearworx, www.handworx.com.au/gearworx/gear.html

National Geographic Kids, kids.nationalgeographic.com/kids

NOVA—Galileo Experiments,
www.pbs.org/wgbh/nova/galileo/experiments.html

PBS Zoom Activities, pbskids.org/zoom/activities/sci/

PBS—The Design Squad, pbskids.org/designsquad/index.html

Pyramid Challenge, www.bbc.co.uk/history/interactive/games/
pyramid_challenge/index_embed.shtml

Simple Machines of COSI, www.cosi.org/files/Flash/simpMach/sm1.swf

The Science of Motion, www.fi.edu/pieces/knox/automaton/simple.htm

MUSEUMS AND SCIENCE CENTERS

California Science Center, www.californiasciencecenter.org/

Carnegie Science Center, www.carnegiesciencecenter.org

Children's Museum of Atlanta, www.childrensmuseumatlanta.org/

Detroit Science Center, www.sciencedetroit.org/

Eli Whitney Museum and Workshop, www.eliwhitney.org

Miami Museum of Science, www.miamisci.org/

Museum of the History of Science, www.mhs.ox.ac.uk/

Museum of Science, www.mos.org/sln/Leonardo/Inventorsworkshop.html

The Carnegie Science Museum, www.carnegiesciencecenter.org/

The Exploratorium, www.exploratorium.edu/

The Museum of Science Industry Chicago, www.msichicago.org

The Franklin Institute Science Museum, www2.fi.edu/

Victoria and Albert Museum—Moving Toys,
www.vam.ac.uk/vastatic/microsites/1482_moving_toys/

A

Abbey of Mont St. Michel, 74
activities
  Boat, 64–65
  Castle Pulley System,
   78–79
  Chopstick Challenge, 24
  Dough rolling, 43
  Experimenting with
   Wedges, 63
  Friction Experiment, 10
  Fruit Top, 45
  Helicopter, 56
  Ice Cream, 30–31
  Jack, 54
  Journal, 8–9
  Jumping Jack, 20–22
  Let's Carve Fruit, 66–67
  Let's Do the Twist, 55
  Let's Lift with Levers, 23
  Lever identification, 15
  Mini Putt Golf
   Challenge, 32
  Mobile, 11
  Movable Pulley, 75
  Moving with Rollers, 41
  New Invention, 84
  Scavenger Hunt, 85
  Screw, 53
  Sewing with Wedges, 65
  Single Pulley Relay, 76
  Ski Slope, 33
  Spinning Top, 44
  Straw balancing, 6
  Working Together, 42–43
aeronautics, 18, 38, 83
agriculture and farming, 3,
  16–17, 60, 62
animals, 19, 59, 62, 66, 74
archaeology, 17, 21,
  36–37, 51
Archimedes, 16, 18, 51–52,
  53, 72
astrolabes, 38
axes, 58

B

balance, 5, 6, 11
balls and bats, 7, 12, 14
bicycles, 6, 15, 34, 39, 40,
  68, 81
block and tackle, 71–72
bolts, 48
bridges, 60, 82
building. *See* construction

C

Canadarm, 18
catapults, 18
China/Chinese, 39, 52, 76
chisels, 58, 60
compound machines, 3
compound pulleys, 71–72
construction, 3, 17, 27,
  60–61, 68, 71, 73, 81, 82
cranes, 17, 68, 70, 71,
  73, 76
cranks, 34, 51

D

da Vinci, Leonardo, 56
Deere, John, 62
defense and weapons, 18,
  27, 59
doorstops, 57, 58
Drais, Karl, 39
drill bits, 49
dump trucks, 14

E

Easter Island, 21
effort, 13–14, 23, 25
Egypt/Egyptians, 3, 14, 16,
  19, 25, 27, 36, 41, 60
elevators, 50, 68, 74
energy, 9, 13–14, 23, 25, 38
engineers, 80–83
equilibrium, 5

F

farming, 3, 16–17, 60, 62
Ferris wheels, 39
fixed pulleys, 70
flags/flagpoles, 2, 68, 70
forces, 4, 5–7, 10, 11, 23, 27,
  50, 55, 57, 69
France/French, 17, 29, 39,
  73, 74
Franklin, Benjamin, 67
friction, 6–7, 10, 50, 55
fulcrum, 13–14, 23, 25

G

gear wheels, 40, 42–43, 48
Goldberg, Rube, 83
golf, 32, 62
gravity, 6, 7, 27
Greece/Greeks, 16, 18, 38,
  51, 72, 73
Gutenberg, Johannes, 52

H

hammers, 25
Hanging Gardens of
Babylon, 51
helicopters, 52, 56
Hero of Alexandria, 19
Hipparchus, 38
human body, 12, 14, 15,
  59, 63
hunting, 3, 59

I

inclined planes, 2, 26–29,
  31, 32, 33.
  See also screws
inventors/inventions,
  80–83, 84

J

jacks/jackscrews,
  49–50, 54

K
knives, 9, 57, 58, 66

L
levers, 2, 12–19, 20, 21, 23, 24, 25, 36.
    See also wheels and axles
linkages, 15
load, 13–14, 25
locks, 28–29

M
mechanical advantage, 1
Meyers, Andrew, 50
movable pulleys, 70–71, 75

N
Nabataeans, 61
nails, 46, 55, 58
needles, 65
Newton, Isaac, 7

O
Otis, Elisha Graves, 50

P
Petra, city of, 61
pliers, 14
plows, 62, 66
pottery wheels, 37–38
printing presses, 52
pulleys, 2, 68–74, 75, 76, 78
pushing/pulling, 4–5, 6–7, 9, 23, 27
pyramids, 3, 27, 41, 60

R
ramps, 2, 6, 26, 27, 31
razor blades, 58, 62
Robertson, Peter Lymburner, 47
rolling pins, 43
Roman Coliseum, 3, 17, 74
Romans, 3, 13, 14, 18, 27, 60, 72, 73–74

S
sailing and ships, 3, 28–29, 38, 64–65, 68, 71–72
scissors, 14
screws, 2, 46–52, 53, 54, 55, 56
seesaws, 12–13
shadufs, 16–17
shovels, 2, 4, 58
Sikorsky, Igor I., 56
simple machines
    common, 2
    forces impacting, 4–7, 10, 11, 23, 27, 50, 55, 57, 69
    inclined planes as, 2, 26–29, 31, 32, 33.
        See also screws
    inventors using, 80–83
    levers as, 2, 12–19, 20, 21, 23, 24, 25, 36.
        See also wheels and axles
    mechanical advantage of, 1
    pulleys as, 2, 68–74, 75, 76, 78
    screws as, 2, 46–52, 53, 54, 55, 56
    wedges as, 2, 57–62, 63, 64–65, 66–67
    wheels and axles as, 2, 34–40, 41, 42–43, 44, 45
Sivrac, Comte de, 39
skiing and snowboarding, 5, 28, 33
sledges, 35, 41
slides, 26, 47
snowplows, 66
spatulas, 62
sports, 5, 7, 12, 14, 15, 26, 28, 32, 33, 62, 67
stairs, 26
swim fins, 67

T
teeth, 59, 63
tow-trucks, 68
toys, 20, 44, 45, 52
trebuchets, 18
Tweels, 40

W
water
    collecting and pumping, 16–17, 19, 51–52, 53
    transportation via, 28–29.
        See also sailing and ships
water wheels, 38, 70
weapons and defense, 18, 27, 59
wedges, 2, 57–62, 63, 64–65, 66–67
wheelbarrows, 4, 14, 39
wheelchairs, 2, 31
wheels and axles, 2, 34–40, 41, 42–43, 44, 45
winding roads, 26–27, 29
windlass, 74
work, defined, 4
worm gears, 48

Z
zip lines, 71, 72
zippers, 2, 62